Self/Pity

Also by Susan Hahn

Harriet Rubin's Mother's Wooden Hand
Incontinence
Confession
Holiday
Mother in Summer

SELF/PITY

SUSAN HAHN

NORTHWESTERN
UNIVERSITY PRESS

Evanston, Illinois

Northwestern University Press
Evanston, IL 60208-4170

Copyright © 2005 by Susan Hahn. Published 2005 by Northwestern
University Press. All rights reserved.

Printed in the United States of America

10   9   8   7   6   5   4   3   2   1

ISBN 0-8101-5164-2 (cloth)
ISBN 0-8101-5165-0 (paper)

Library of Congress Cataloging-in-Publication Data

Hahn, Susan.
   Self/pity / Susan Hahn.
      p. cm.
      ISBN 0-8101-5164-2 (cloth : alk. paper) — ISBN 0-8101-5165-0
   (pbk. : alk. paper)
      I. Title.
   PS3558.A3238S45 2005
   811'.54—dc22

2005010139

FOR JACOB

My mother groan'd! my father wept:
Into the dangerous world I leapt:
Helpless, naked, piping loud:
Like a fiend hid in a cloud.

"Infant Sorrow," William Blake

Contents

Six

Acknowledgments

Grateful acknowledgment is made to the editors of the following publications, in which these poems, or versions of them, first appeared:

American Poetry Review: "Goose Pity"

Boulevard: "The Seventh Chakra"

Kenyon Review: "Pity the Self—Middle-aged"

Michigan Quarterly Review: "O Baby O"

New England Review: "Pity Dance for a Small Troupe," "Pity Jerusalem," "Pity the Judas Tree," "Pity Song in Solo Voice without Accompaniment"

Ninth Letter: "Pity the Brain," *from* "The Pornography of Pity," parts IV and V

Poetry: "Pity the Skin," "The Pity of Punctuation"

Tikkun: "For Jacob Four Months in the Womb"

I am forever indebted to the John Simon Guggenheim Memorial Foundation, whose award of a fellowship allowed me the time to complete this book.

Self/Pity

ONE

O Baby O

Rock-a-bye, baby,
On the tree top . . .

Random movements so high
in the uterine tube—
an overheated breeze blown
in, the world all gelatin,
a slow swim up, then
more cleaving to the lining
of this world. The top, topped
with life—excitable bud
swelling—everything connecting,
a tiny branching
bush, blood bathing
its twigs, suspended in

a watery fluid, the embryo
holds its shape, molds
its body on the tree—
O tree of life—ablaze
in the garden swing
of the woman trying
to temper her own tempo,
while soon baby will
rock to his own
O Baby O.

When the wind blows,
The cradle will rock . . .

In the neural groove
an unsung song sings on,
the notochord enough
backbone to hold
the silent strum against
the quiet breeze.
The cradle understands its own

determination. The heart
precociously forms its *thump,*
thump, thump announcement,
while stalked eye cups
and impocketing inner ears
begin to locate the which way
of the wind. The fetus face facing
forward to face whatever—
the outside world weather
of little matter. Now,

he can almost hear the hum
of himself—interior music
he slowly curls around to become
O Baby O.

When the bough breaks,
The cradle will fall . . .

Fig tree encircling natal mahogany.
Camel thorn with weaverbird nests.
Spruce and alder forest.
Southern beeches, winter frost.
Swamp cypress. Baobab. Olive.
Brittle gum. Coconut palms.
Live oak. Quiver tree. Fever tree. Ash.
Leaf with drip tips. Weeping willow.
Everywhere the breaking.
O Baby O.

And down will come baby,
Cradle and all.

Downward, groundward, the forces
of the waters push the back
of the head forward. Soon all seas
of earth—rain, sleet, and snow
and those that have dried and hardened
to blister color—will be seen.
Against the sloping wall
a rotating goes on to a rhythm—
meeting all resistance as a ferryboat
shunted into its wharf.
The boatman across the river,

drunk on today's coins,
sways and jingles
in his vertigo at the edge
of his turf, chuckles
O Baby O.

Two

Pity the Foot

Forlorn in its sole
with its thick pad of fat
that isn't ample enough
to really protect
any inner part
from the pressure on it—
jar of the earth
when it quakes
open, hike over broken
bodies of rock, the slip
on the snow-covered mirror,
deceptively pure. Elastic
spring of the arch

never to rise high enough
to fly off this planet—
that's left to the soul
with no bones attached,
which no one can draw.
Foot, heavier than hand
but with less freedom,
doesn't even try to imagine
such illustrations,

just hopes not to get hurt
as it moves along.

Pity the Appendix

Impotent gut worm, at its best
when quiet—reminder of what I
once was—*low creature
of inflammation,* on all fours—
all pant in June,
palms flat to floor
(hot stink of the unwashed
slats, with the sun at its apex)
and knees there too, all cut—
my ancient animal call, the beg
of the crawl. Then, on two feet, my *caw,
caw, caw.* How obsolete, *old crow*

in the drought meadow rage—
swamp puss—this pain
of doubling up of
heart to stomach, stomach to heart
of disgust.

And the Hindgut

Past the eternal pith of talk,
down the entry pit of mouth,
through the basket with its complex
bars of bone that holds the lump
heart, lies all baseness

of thought. Here, the comedian drops
dumb jokes—his puns of double dirt—
or the philosopher runs on
with his dribble of green
meaning—the essence of the detritus
held in his moist palm—
while the unexamined life spits out

the broadcaster's mouth or splashes the starlet on,
covering her own star
with just a thong, eventually to be
tossed off like wet confetti
after the party. After the party

the autonomic shock
of nerves and blood reeks
the pink. Eye and end
of the idea that can only be realized
in the rancid.

Pity the Skin

The Stoics would not have touched this bite,
would have let it swell into all misery
of skin—the burn that goes past blister,

the defiant rough-edged wart,
the scleroderma that reaches down
and insists on the final
constriction of the heart. *Ignore*

these nerve endings—all endings. The "I"
says to the "me"—too sensitive to cold
(your back) and heat (his wild grab dig).
The Stoics demanded repentance—said God
could not be moved
by pity. How hard and dry

to blood cracks and scaly crust
is the inflammation on the caps of knees on wood.
The lice and scabies mites keep coming
to play on the surface
and in the depths
of the wanderer who can't resist
the itch of getting lost.

Pity the Face

Vision, smell, and taste
lock into a small space.
Eyes, nose, and mouth
immature, miniature with the minuscule
afterimage of the muzzle—the clump
that protruded into, intruded
on every stump of land.
The front of the head, now

more delicate, will lead
with its heart—future
blood place to be bled—
but first the face faces out,
pushes with all its strength
its striated muscles into
the flushed world and, startled,
sees enlarged nasal tunnels,
a quick eruption of teeth—
called a smile. And the child
in the crib looks up at this mobile—

all spins of emotions—
that will twirl into poem,
story, novel—all plays
with their articulations
of *tragedy* and its sputtering half-
cousin *pity*, who keeps
tripping for attention.

Pity the Brain

It is the unexpected burst
into ignorance, mistake—the loss
of the fatty substance—discretion—
when the longitudinal fissure widens
so one thought is as disconnected
from another as the separation of oceans—
the land between parched and all actions or re-
actions wandering the desert of the formidable
cacti, braille that bleeds the fingertips
to unreadable. *Your behavior and mine*
untouchable and, thereby, indecipherable.
Dragged down, the body's grooves

chewed and dumped, the brain surrenders
all barriers—all safeguards—and the blood bleeds
into tissue no MRI can figure. All machines—
leaden weights—search the cloudy matter
for answers that matter. Same as the philosophers
with their own limits, because all power
resides elsewhere. *You*

relegate my behavior to split
(SPIT?) AND SHOUT—an excess
or deficiency of chemicals, yet allow
me my ecstasies and obsessions,
my inflammations when confronting
contradictory instructions. *That bird brain*

trapped in its small room
of bone, crashing into all walls.
It's really so unseemly

to be pitied.

Pity the Self—Middle-aged

Lying in the body is the self, lying
to everyone that it's *great*—bloated
insomniac homunculus—rolling
in the ruins of the layered
skin and spin of fat, sneaking
tidbits at night from self-
help books beside itself
for help—a quick fix to grasp
a little rest, find its *spirit path*—
a Hindu Veda written in Sanskrit

would be nice—
far away from all craving,
the itch of carbohydrate scratch,
of want and hypothesis.
The refrigerator is packed
with cuts of cold
hopes that still desire to be grabbed
and heated—*stuffed self*

with its empty heart, its thickening
waist. Soon the waste of the body will
temporarily rid itself from the weight
of the noisy liar and the lair
of *Here Me, Hear Me.* The wish:

no more migrations from one birth
to the next—*through all hungers of the ages,
to be lifted from such bondage.*

Pity Such Teeth

Reptilian with their sharp backward twist,
they swallow unexamined
constructions. Ill-planned whole
paragraphs slung upon other fallen run-on
sentences, create a putrid body
of thought. *Gossip.* How lost

the words are as they are nicked
and tumble down to the bowel pit,
though sometimes their careen is slowed,
caught between large flat grinding
ridges with cusps—low mastications—
the hyperflux of undoing and doing over
the undone. All belch and roil
going on ad nauseam
for those who come close enough
for the whiff and then the autonomic
gasp away. We have lost

our sweet milk teeth—
pure babies of form and delight.
They lie under the pillow left
for Mother to discover, Mother
who lies under the mouth—
that ice-white enameled
mud-stump of decay.
In *that* winter

we'll be like the birds
with no real teeth,
just muscular gizzards—
all hunger and hope, chirp-talk—
and wait for the tongue's complete
extinction—all sound finally bound
to the floor of the inexpressible ground.

Pity the Self—Postmortem

Autopsy

All taboos erased against opening
the body that has ceased
to move, the Y-shaped incision—
deep as the *WHY?* of the family
in the next room crying to the torn
photograph—is made,
extending from the armpits
and carried beneath
the breast to the bottom of the sternum,
then continuing down to the lower
abdomen where the groin meets
the lifeless sex. Soon all

studies—toxicological, bacteriological, and viral—
will be able to determine the scientific
WHY? And all organs will be returned,
all incisions carefully sewn with no unseemly

evidence of the disruption, while the self
wanders outside, lonely, waiting its turn
to go back home—invisible
to the body and the weeping family.

dECAY

All composure softens
to marsh and gas—swamp
of skin the self drifts in
as it tries to grab on to any bone,
an incisor locked within the jaw, anything incisive
it can call home. After the punch
of numbers, the phone is not picked up,
so the message plays on and on, the litany
of a singular voice breaking down

elsewhere into something simpler, the air
is so full of the circular—
all molecules being returned
to the atmosphere, while the self slips
down, down to behind the sacrum,
asks the soul to wipe it, cleanse it,
and begs to be taken along.

Pity the Self—Postmodern

Nothing to hang itself on—
all the absolutes split
nails rusting the cells
of martyrs who marched
the jagged past to un-

embodied Jerusalem. How malleable
the clay spirit, the sooty body—
twisted as a pipe cleaner,
the pineal gland a squashed pea
unable to control its own

history. The field is piled high
with the damaged
images—the sects, the uniforms—
each team's letters,
shredded. The self searches

an early text and another prior
to that—can't stop
trying to find its reference
point. *Point of no return. What is
the point?* In the confessional
everything was so direct—

the helping of forgiveness,
a Passover Seder
heaped onto the plate,
the Angel of Death not

touching it. Now, eat
from it—and feel
the doubled-over
full dry heave of emptiness.

THREE

The Seventh Chakra

The forefinger and thumb thrum
on the odd feel of the short stiff hairs
like those found on a hog or a hat
of felt—*press and mat*
to the crown. That place

the sun hits first and the moon hides from
and the soul tries to crack
from its skull shell
like a newborn chick.
All the pushing in, the pushing out,
make the wound
so callous
yet always opening,
opening up to the opening
of the death of the dance:
the coulda, woulda, shoulda rumba
of the overexposed, over-
heated. Suddenly it's too bright
to move—play at any game, even
golf—too hot—for the precise positioning
of the hands on *that* stick—
the *putt, putt, putt* into that
tiny bald hole. A larger one insists on being

dug, the thick shovel handled
by thug fists. It's time
for the scorch of silence—
all focus on the delicate lotus
that has fought to emerge
from the moth-ravaged head.

ANd iTS piTY STORY . . .

Start (or end) with the space below
the sacrum. Spine all
strength and bounce before
Mother gave you the filthy book
that so many had drooled over,
taken beneath the covers.
Remember how you read about the dogs
and knew even then the stink
and heft of that kind of love
would find you. On the height
of the genitals with their open petals
all earth—all raw
material—how you crumbled

while you waited for his call. And when
he finally did and said *over-*
slept (WITH WHOM?) and, now, had
misplaced his wallet—could you *pay, pay, pay*
for dinner? And all of this way

after you left the one you dressed in white for
and walked down *that* aisle pit. His base
chakra a slime of honey
on the moon. *O honey-*
moon, where you got glued to a high

fever and he dragged you in-
to the cartographer's room and penned
his own map into your body.
No illusions left and no reason
ever to allude to any hell

29

in any myth. The self-
made journey enough
in the labyrinth

of Las Vegas—town of craps,
blackjack, and screw-
drivers—Oh, sticky mess
of vodka over the orange
when it spilled *on the honey-
moon.* Clutching a stained

ivory silk pillow
to your navel—mangled wound
from where the cord was cut,
was supposed to separate you
from the womb—you returned
any which way home,
never again to be impressed
by anyone's trip. All knowledge
bitten from the forced

swallow of the sick apple,
the pain hit and hit all
lower muscles and you curled
around a cushion of muted
hysteria and rocked
into the dark with the help of Nembutal
which you stole from your mother's night-

stand and the womb wandered
and there was no wonder, no light,
for the moon hid behind every cloud
it could find, fevered
in its hypochondriac malaria,

from its own view
of the world—sometimes feeling
like a helpless voyeur stuck there.

And the third chakra shut. The mouth
of the stomach just wanting, *wanting*
sugar dripped into it. And you filled
your pockets with lemon Life-
Savers and watched them dig

someone your age into April—
that fleshy ground when everything
is supposed to grow up
and out and you screamed into that mound pillow
Why not me? And your parents did not
hug you. Just said,
please be quiet, while the heart
chakra with the twelve petals
closed and all oceans of sentiment dried up
as you crossed over—all attachments
relinquished, at least momentarily—
and you fingered the waxy green twine
that releases the Life-
Savers. All prayer over,

you left her to the moon
with its slivered stare
until a vertigo set in and you spun
out of control and talked to anyone
who would and would not
listen, even while you slept and dreamed
of a place with lots of lawn.

The Third Eye Winking There,
or was it just the pubescent
half-moon playing peekaboo with you,
readying itself for its own bloat—*O
honey on the moon*—
its gaze, so gooey when full-
blown on impure things, *on
you.* And you

locked yourself in your room,
yet a fragile gate kept
swinging open—a very pointed
picket fence on which you dug
letters, then words, and they anointed
your crown—*that moth hole*—
and the moon yelled down
*No. No. No.
You Cannot Be In Possession,
Only Be Possessed.* And you

grew so deaf to its motions
and turned and turned and turned
from the tricky honey moon,
spread the hair on your head
to the darkness—allowed it in—
and felt the bloom of the lotus.
The lemon LifeSavers—the world—
rolling, dissolving, on your tongue.

FOUR

The Pornography of Pity

I

I am so curious for just one more bite—

one more round with the arrow pointed
at the Pandora's box that lifts
the lid of the eye—the "I"—
one more downward
try to see more. *Is there anything
we should not know?*
The pity inside

the jar the god sent
with the modest maiden was a gift
of grief and cares and the beautiful
evil—the femme
fatale and the bitch goddess who cuts
a broad swath of corruption. Always

a woman who ends up
the whore quite common
and wrong—wronged(?)—as I
punch in the forbidden childhood
word and on the turned-on
screen out pops pictures
of *Oh My Gosh, Oh*

*Yes. O Zeus
how you have truly hurt us.*

II

I cannot stop accessing the site—

my sight fixed on the woman
on her back, the three men
satisfying themselves on her.
Because she is so unlovely
I keep thinking how hungry
she must have been to have shown
herself so chewed on. *At midnight*

how the eyes flame into
the brain's latched chamber. Psyche,
not resisting prying open
another box warned against
tampering with, was overcome

by a Stygian sleep—
better than Lot's wife,
who turned toward soot-
filled Sodom for one
last glance. Once,

the Earth was one
language, temptation contained
in a jar, the apple shined
on the tree under the new morning sun,
the woman lay naked on the grass
joined only to nature's green—

pity had not yet sprawled
itself onto the known
sheets, the forbidden had not yet
crawled into a room so dimly lit.

III

Onstage is one God, two
humans of the opposite sex,
two trees bursting at the edge
of the garden set, the audience, still
innocent, sits quiet—
attends to the play—
watches the desire

to know more conquer the immortal.
By the door a psychiatrist snores—
he's tired of analyses he doesn't
get paid for. The serpent
appears, the unexplained land-

lord—a crumb of love and pity
on the tip of his tongue.
He knows he's in
control of what's to come,
has his timing down—
rehearsed and rehearsed
his line—under-
stands the power of its coil
into the cerebellum,
then the payment
from the tenants—
the split between

the Holy and the Pollutant.
The audience's reaction forever now
the insistence of repentance. How hard
they applaud. Their skin so raw, their minds
convex. *The psychiatrist*
wakes up. He's missed it all.

The others exit
the hall cradling the odious off-
spring of Satan's incest
with Sin—the child
who will never let them rest.
The child the psychiatrist cannot explain,

the child with the same beginning and end
name we come to know
to call Death.

IV

If discretion is the undoing,
then I am hardly undone.
If, however, breaking
a prohibition begins the un-
raveling into knowledge,

I am out there—out
on the not so strong,
perhaps the weakest, limb.
The quest motif, I guess,
is in—in the hook in-

to the how-to book, the map
to the treasure is in
my awkward hands, I lope
along reading it—the path blocked
by only the unridden
wooden horses I bump
into and try to rearrange. *Is language
that (un)movable?* From noble

knight to knavish picaro.
Don Quixote went harmlessly mad.
It's in the *harmless* that lies
the trouble. If it is
harmless, how can it be mad?
And if it is, all madness
will come as bliss rushes

through the door flung open
by the jocular trickster.
*My native town is no longer enough,
yet the far side is so crowded*

with discontents—so clean
and dressed up, their minds
a tatter. The quid pro quo of the soul
exchanged for a time
of magic; how we travel
in herds carrying coins
that will only end up
in the boatman's pocket
and finally as anchors
on our lids. Certainly

the payment for knowledge cannot be
argued with and is
being dealt with in high places.
Isn't it? It is our chorus.

(PAUSE i)

Be lowly wise
Archangel Raphael to Adam

Today, I will not trip
the downward path
toward wisdom. Today,
there is no need
for pity. Today, withdrawal

pulls me into my starched corner
where neither Prometheus nor Pandora fits.
It is so safe here
in my chair with my pen and paper.
Today, imagination is the only
imaginable answer—no question
marks from anyone to hang myself
on and pierce the body to blood.
No mess to wipe up.
Outside my window the apple
is only visible in my peripheral vision,
although it's easy
to see how the wind excites it.
Today, I know there is a limit

to my reach. Today,
this is the only thing
that touches me.

V

How sad the scientists are tonight
in their underground tombs;
they have known the siren song,
their minds rhapsodized by the high-
pitched tune.

We've come so far not to come along.

How sad the scientists are tonight—
their proud knowledge, the mud
that now cuddles them.
Once, it was a garden

so clean and bright
(no, no, not *that* one).
One tended by delicate monk hands—
twenty years of legumes grown
and noted with green reverence—
peeling to naked discovery
what was dominant, what was
recessive. While in the hidden forest, chaos

lusted over peaceful rhythm—
monsters' mammoth feet plunged
into the dust of the quietly curious,
stole, then strangled their song.

We've come so far not to come along.

VI

How sad the old sadist,
his eyes shrouded from the sun
with thick-rimmed, darkened shades
that hide his limp wink and leer.
How sad the old sadist, gripping

his whip with weak strength—
a reckless jerk and rip
on the upper, inner quick
curve cut of his still-perfect calves—
now marked. Sad old sadist
with all the equip-

ment and so few words left to spit.
The Marquis is in. The Marquis is out.
The shout, the slap, the scream,
the blast of flesh always
an attraction and afterward
always the coming not

of calm but the crash birthing
of mutations, the mottled, bent
hand, now, on the overexamined
skin—old worm holes—
that he, exhausted,
brushes by and sags
away from.

VII

Sorry Sade I say. I do
not feel sad for you
nor would you care me
to, which is even
sadder than the saddest
path that self-pity
ever rode on bare-
backed, bare, back on
abstract concepts—

poetic trots of no responsibility.
But this is not your ordinary cross-
word puzzle, cross in
the road, cross mad-
woman, crossing herself, genu-
flecting to the timid wind.
This is the real thump and crash
and bruise and bash over
the stone-strewn road
that no hooves will not crack over.
This is the nature that convulses

Over. Over
is what Sade said in bed.
Over. Over. Please Turn
Over. A new leaf(?)
one that does not grow
on the erotic tree
with its flash and ram-
ifications? Forget It.
Turn. Turn. Turn
and do not look back.
(This is worse, I thought, than turning

44

to salt with its awful pillar taste,
this lull in the lull-
a-by as I lie stunned, still.)
Good-bye, Sade said. *GOOD-BYE,*
he shouted bare-
backed, bareback
when so easily he galloped off.

(PAUSE ii)

Outside my window the sounds *cheer-up,*
cheer-up sing spring. A pair
of robins are gathering materials.
The female finds a tree
of life—not knowledge—
selects a branch and weaves
weeds and twigs and rags and string
with bits of mud that dry like glue,
then adds more mud and presses it
with her breast into a cup shape
and lines it with a bed of grass.
All is so strong and safe and snug.
She sits so proud. *He* sings

so loud a warning for others
to stay away. And they do.
Soon four new robins hatched from the blue
squawk for food as their warm down feathers
grow hard enough to fly them
from the nest, from the hover of the tree,
but not from this nature that I watch.

VIII

I am Alice, Alice fallen
into the rabbit hole. I am
Didi and Gogo waiting—waiting
for Godot. Are there things I should
not know—the cosmic joke?
The *horror vacui?* What a wonderland

of curiosity fixates the eye on the apple.
Oh, for a bite of pure
disinterested delight. *Can I Kant?*
O Mother May I? Her voice
no longer gives permission, a path out.
The tweezer is hidden—the one needed
to pluck the unwanted gnarled weeds.
Just the teasers are left to pull
my right arm onto the cobbled, motley road.
A rogue whispers the password—
experiment. But aside from his heft
and sweat, his smash against
my body, can he grasp
what I long to hold—
the tiniest and largest of what
is the infinite? Two steeds

still draw the sun across my sky.
Yet, the temptation of Icarus burns
my heart—the flame of the unlived
life, the chance of it,
makes of me a voyeur
of my neighbor, watching
strangers come and go,
the record plays in my room—repetitions

of "Don't Fence Me In" punctuate
my skin. How many piercings
of the heart until it stops
bleeding? Pity all histories
of hormones and lunge,
all yearnings to give Mr. Hyde
one more chance. The road
Mother lies under is so riddled
with riddles. Gone is
rocking me to dream with *High*

Diddle Diddle,
the Cat and the Fiddle,
the Cow Jumped over the Moon,
and the Dish Ran Away with the Spoon.
No sleep comes anymore with
the absurd, the bed impossibly rumpled.
The ghoul always lurking—

shadow in the room's sloped corner,
blending with the tree, crawled
into every crevice—trying to convince
me that it is possible to know it all.
If I would just obey, he promises

to teach me how to *really* spin
each piece of straw into gold.

Five

The Pity of Punctuation

Hoard of words released like manic
spring with its quick gush blooms of bright
where endings have not even a small chance
life forever resurrecting itself without the monster
splotch which when shrunken to depressed
the psychoanalyst calls the period
of realization and the patient hangs on
for her dear however listless
existence like a hyphen at the end
of its rope searching for its dropped
letters like I wait and hold my breath
for my letter that the male carrier might bring
with the possible swerve of love
before any wall of stiff brackets
and the unforgiving is embedded
into the type you know the type

where false hope lies in the dash and never forget

the pun how could one for therein
lived the fun when it was lost inside
me as my body and all punctuation
was temporarily erased eight years ago
same as the symbol of eternity
in April that whore month
with its hoard of all that is
possible while the sun slowly pitched itself
into the lake and he left and suddenly

too many commas crawled in carrying
colons with their screaming litanies of lists
and question marks with *WHYWHYWHY*
on their small hooked spineless backs
and the parade would not stop

until finally the period did roll in so bleak
and yet what a tiny thing it *was*
as I began to feel the fade into
the seamless midnight sky
with my being given
no choice but to curve onto that dot
and disappear with it

Goose Pity

Old Mother Goose,
When she wanted to wander,
Would ride through the air
On a very fine gander.

In the nursery the walls are bare
and cracked to half split open.
The rocking chair has disappeared
as has the goosey blanket.
The rhymes have fractured and flaked
on the window frames and the moth-
eaten curtains beg to be cut off
from all memories of kings
and pies and blackbirds baked
alive, of spiders crawling
into fabric and old women
tossed up in a blanket
"to brush the cobwebs
off the sky." Mother lies

six years in the cabbage patch
of dirt and thorn and though I tear
through the involuted, untamed path
in May, July, October,
I never go deep enough
to find her, hear her, warn her
that the room is a ruin,
has been turned
upside down. Show her the twist

of my skeleton
face, how I chew on
the memory of the bill knob
of the disappeared swan
(the book called it the perfect
aphrodisiac) so I can forget the longing,
how he really did come to call,
rubbed oil from right above
his tail to maintain
his gorgeous plumage.
Too stained we both became—
aslither in preening.
How we'd dip and pump—
wings all expanse—
pinioned only to each other.
Late frosts and early floods
were the weather of *not yet.* True,
the crows and gulls, snails and foxes,
drooled and waited and watched
as inevitably

I did for him.
Took up with others,
fixated on the changing designs
of their beaks, their thick fleshy
tongues—*surf scoter, king eider,*
horned screamer—always hoping
for the soughing creak of wings
of the lone mute swan.
Talk, talk to me, I'd plead

to the ignorant forest
that, unlike him or Mother, answered.

Goosey, goosey gander,
Whither shall I wander?
Upstairs and downstairs,
And in my lady's chamber.

It was the stiff flight feathers,
the down underneath,
that I can't forget.
How he swam into me, all
grace—the white-blur flutter.
Some days I remember him
as huckster, trickster, monster;
others as the god transformed, zeroing
in on me—the waiting, blazing center.
How mythic. How cliché.
Either way. Better than OK.
Woo. Wound. Woe. Whoa.
I'd scream too loud
How strange, so he found
another—quieter—and now
I find him only
for certain, filling up my page.

Riddle me, riddle me, what is that
Over my head and under my hat?

She read me rhymes in the nursery
as I watched the flicker
of her hand pick out her hair—
one by one, rub the inflamed emptiness
to message—scabs I could examine.
Animal skin I could learn from—
parchment unscrolled by tiny fingers
with secret world maps—
translucent, simple, readable
under the porcelain bird
lamp—terrain so navigable
it would travel me into calm.

Gray goose and gander
Waft your wings together
And carry the good king's daughter
Over the one-strand river.

Six

Pity Dance for a Small Troupe

Tonight the churchyard crowds
with too many legs flung to sky,
thudded to ground. Some hit the stones
that cover the tombs
creating more flesh to wound to lesion.
A tarantella plays on—
the spiders for now have gone underground.
The bodies above are sweating it out—
all vaccine gone. All that's left

is the music for purposeless motion—
a time for diffuse blushes
on trunk or limb
before the killing deep
hemorrhagic rash sets in.
In the near distance

wild rodents and fleas dance
hidden away, choreographing a plague.

Pity Song in Solo Voice without Accompaniment

How quiet the stretched skin over
the singular body—its coo and hum
and minute beat on the planet
crust. The mattress
is so bumpy and sunk,
squeaking on—sad song

sing-a-long to a distant memory
of a ram's-horn trumpet inside
the temple's walls. *Sing to me,*

said the woman to the man
and just a hollow column of air appeared,
begged the man to his god,
and just one plucked string was heard,
cried the child in his crib. *So I did*

something spontaneous, I then forgot.
Afterward, we slept all
coo and hum, only the child
firm on the words he dreamed on.

EVERYONE

Who walks the Way of Sorrows now
quiet, travels alone bare-
footed, touching Jerusalem stone? After

the Eucharist, the epithets
(*El Elyon, El Olam, El Bethel*),
the hymns, the hums, a volumed silence
builds into an outrageous tinnitus.
The bells will not stop—
the world planet head a banging
of forehead to floor for forgiveness.
All frescoes of ascensions, long finished,

peel and crack. God leaves
returns, but does not come back.
The Ark a portable palladium.
In the Cenacle on the Mount of Zion—
Dome of Rock—there once was a moment

(*wasn't there? probably not.*)
no one yet drunk—
no one yet violent.
No blood splotched a neighbor's back-
yard. Now, he tries not to look out,
busies himself inside hanging
lights on a dreamy

pink plastic tree, an angel
affixed to the top of it. *Sings.*

Everyone wants to get to heaven
on its nailed-down, delicate wings.

Pity Jerusalem

City of too many Sabbaths
that sleeps with one eye shut,
the other open, checking
if the gate is locked. Too many

donkeys and push-
carts roll down the narrow streets,
hauling the dead
to their respective gods.
Site of Supper and Sacrifice—
ascensions to heaven from
a cross or a stone—
a bullet, a message jammed
into the crevice of the body-broken
wall—*always the craving to reach*

God in this desert of deserted
space, where prayer rises
and falls like a cloud
come to fog. How many
amulets can be sold,
stuffed into pockets, hung on
necks thrust forward, looking
apish! How many clawed feet

can dig into an inch of land
until it gives itself up and caves in?

Pity the Judas Tree

I say

I sold my love
for thirty coins
and, as they weighted down
my pockets, gave him
a kiss to carry on
the saddest cobbled path.
Then, with the hammered, polished
metal, I bought myself a soft field
to lie in, the opposite of the rusted nails
and splintered wood my love
would die on.

They say

I hung my tortured heart on a tree
filled with the dazzle of rose-pink petals.
And now, my soul twirls
in hell's deepest chasm
with Julius Caesar's assassins.

I say

I was just a part of the pitiful
plan. Just like you
I acted like
me. It's all the same story
of temptation.

Whatever you say

Don't you see
victim's evil, once again,
taught a lesson in the full
bloom beauty of a tree?

For Jacob Four Months in the Womb

Now that you can stretch, distinguish
sweet from bitter, now that
your eyes are sensitive
to light and you are able
to move and shield yourself
from too much bright,
be watchful of the gleaming

angel. Fugitive, wanderer, peddler—
we are all with our little star
to pander for a flicker.
But, forever he
has come along, he who lasts
and laughs and burns
out our hearts, our pitiful
right. So remember to keep

climbing, climbing up the rungs
of the ladder made of rope,
made of wood, made of metal—
whatever the material you make
of it in your womb dreams.
Angels are circling
around you. And when the boldest
appears and says *I have hold of you,*

wrestle him with your clean foot.
Fight all night as the stunned
moon stares down, gives

you its timid glow, and the wind
moves the branches to song.
*Ask For The Blessing. Ask
For It Now.* Before

you enter the burnt-out garden.
Hold it tight in your right
hand as you pass through
the flooded gate into
the land that lies fallow.
*Remind us again and again
how you fought off the angel.*

About the Author

Susan Hahn is a poet, a playwright, and the editor of
TriQuarterly magazine. She is the author of five books of
poetry and the recipient of many awards for her poems,
including a Guggenheim Fellowship in 2003. The *Chicago
Tribune* named her fourth book, *Holiday,* and her fifth
book, *Mother in Summer,* among the best books of 2002.
Her first play, *Golf,* premiered in 2005.